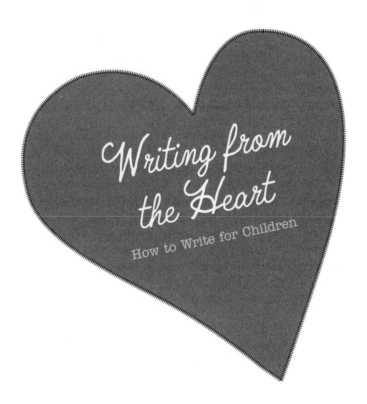

Writing from the Heart

How to Write for Children

*This book is dedicated to Dr Libby Limbrick
for all that she has done for the children of New Zealand.*

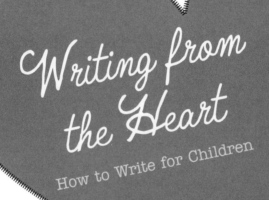

Writing from the Heart

How to Write for Children

Storylines
Children's Literature Charitable Trust

BOYDS MILLS PRESS
Honesdale, Pennsylvania

Boyds Mills Press, Inc.
815 Church Street
Honesdale, Pennsylvania 18431
Printed in the United States of America
First U.S. edition, 2011

ISBN: 978-1-59078-871-4 (hc) • ISBN: 978-1-59078-802-8 (pb)

Library of Congress Control Number: 2011925878

Originally published in 2010 by
Storylines Children's Literature Charitable Trust of New Zealand
PO Box 96 094
Balmoral, Auckland 1342, New Zealand
www.storylines.org.nz

Editors: Peter Dowling, Tessa Duder
Designer: Kate Walters—Dynamac Publishing Services, Ltd.
Illustrator: Fraser Williamson

CONTENTS

iNTRODUCTiON

This is not a book of instruction but rather a sharing of long experience as a writer, an editor and a facilitator of writing workshops. I hope you will read it as such and relate it to your own writing. If what I say doesn't connect with your experience, let it go. I discovered a long time back that I could never receive suggestions unless I was ready for them.

For me, making stories has been like breathing. It seems that I have always done it, first in pictures, story drawing on any clear space I could find — walls, endpapers of books, tablecloths, sketches on a pavement with a piece of brick — an obsessive habit that did not always please my parents. I was a late reader, nine before I acquired sufficient skills to access story in books, but once that happened, my own story-making changed medium, and I drew pictures with words instead of crayons. I also told stories every night to my sisters, recycling plots from the books I read.

When I was ten, my first story was published in the children's page of the *Southern Cross* newspaper. Six years later, I was the editor of the children's page of the *Manawatu Daily Times*, an after-school job my teachers at Palmerston North Girls' High

School found for me so that I could stay at school and at the same time earn badly needed money for my parents. When I left school at the end of the sixth form, one of those teachers made me promise that I would not give up writing.

A pharmacy apprenticeship, marriage and babies intervened, but I did keep that promise and began writing short stories that were published in various magazines: *Straight Furrow*, *The Listener*, *New Zealand Home Journal*, *Landfall*, *Short Story International*. A New York editor at Doubleday asked if I had a novel. Doubleday eventually published five of my novels for adults, but at the same time I was writing stories for children, especially for my son Edward and others like him who were reluctant readers. Following that was a growing commitment to early reading.

Over the last 40 years I've written about 650 early reading books, and have been involved with the layout and production side of most of them. As well, there have been about 50

picture books, 80 short chapter books and a dozen novels, all of them for children. Kindly teachers have permitted me to do research in their classrooms. Publishers in the United States, New Zealand, Hong Kong and Singapore have had me in their offices to do editorial work. For 16 years I was on the faculty of the Highlights Summer Writing School in Chautauqua, New York, and I have done weekend writing workshops in Alaska, Seattle, Arizona and California in the US, as well as in Malaysia, Singapore, Hong Kong, Brunei, South Africa, Iceland and New Zealand.

The material in this book has come from the sum of this experience.

There is repetition of some key points in *Writing from the Heart*. I feel it necessary to repeat these because of their importance, and because some writers may read only those chapters that relate to their genre.

I hope you find some of it useful. Most of the quotes in it are from my own work, simply to save the hassle of getting permission to quote from other writers. You will have other quotes that will be meaningful to you.

Above all, enjoy your craft. Do keep your serious adult voice under control, and let the child within you grow wings to fly with the child out there. Writing for children is a very satisfying adventure.

Joy Cowley
Wellington, May 2010

1. PLOT

What is plot?

I was with a group of seven- and eight-year-old authors who were comparing notes on writing. Questions and answers went back and forth, and someone mentioned plot.

'What is plot?' I asked, not expecting a reply. They were, after all, very young.

Up shot a hand, and a small boy said, 'It's a kind of problem that gets solved.'

Well, I've seen some long and convoluted adult definitions of plot, but that's about as clear as it comes. Plot is some kind of problem that gets solved. In a plot something happens and the resolution of that happening comes at the end of the story. It's so simple, and yet we can miss it. Sometimes we write stories with plots so slight they don't hold the weight of words we put on them. Or we write stories that have themes but virtually no plot at all.

And here is another definition for you. This time it came from a high school writing class, students of 14 and 15. I asked them, 'What is the difference between theme and plot?'

Back came the reply, 'The theme is what the story is about and the plot is what happens.'

Again, this is a very clear definition. I can write something for children on the theme of patriotism, loneliness, greed, kindness. I can write on the theme of celebration — Hanukkah, Christmas, a birthday party. But theme is not plot. Plot is what happens within this theme. And if there is no plot, I do not have a story. I have an essay, or a vignette. Plot is essential to story. It gives the story its movement.

Now, stories have different lengths, according to the complexity of the plot and the number of characters. On one hand, we might have a 300-word text for a picture book for pre-school children. Another idea might lead to a 30,000-word novel for young adults.

Every idea dictates its format and its length. But whatever we are writing, the plot will carry the movement of the story.

Novels require more complex plotting, but at the moment, let us imagine that we are writing a story for younger readers. We are looking at the traditional three-part story — beginning, middle, end. All of these are concerned with the unravelling of the plot, but we use the arbitrary divisions to describe how we deal with the plot — the way we pace it.

The beginning of the story introduces characters and setting. It lifts the curtain on the stage and brings out the actors. It's in the beginning of the story that we set up all those props we are going to need for the story. For example, if your character is going to escape by picking the lock of a door with a pocket knife, some mention of the pocket knife needs to come early in the story. Generally, the reader feels cheated if we introduce these elements as coincidence near the end. So, in effect, the beginning of the story can be compared with a musical overture. It gives the reader a good deal of information and the enticement to read on. But it is also introducing the main action of the story.

The pace of the beginning is sometimes slowed with description. When pacing our plot, we remember that adjectives and long sentences will slow down the action. Verbs and shorter sentences will increase the speed. As we move into the middle of the story, the part where it is all happening, we use language to match the pace. The easier style of the early structure picks up speed. In the most dramatic part of our story, our language is terse, almost breathless. But this doesn't mean that the big dramatic moment in a story should be dealt with briefly. All too often this happens. As readers we spend a long time getting to the 'crunch' of the tale only to discover that it is dealt with in two sentences. If my character falls from a yacht into a rough sea, I cheat the reader if I state baldly that he fell in the sea and was nearly drowned. I can pan that action out, maybe over one or two pages, giving a terse and fast-moving account of my character's struggles. After all, this is the main action in the story. I must not dismiss it or trivialise it.

We come to the end of our story. The drama has been resolved. There has been a well-constructed solution to the problem. The pace of the language can be relaxed. This final wind-up is brief and it leaves the reader feeling satisfied.

At this point we might look at the beginnings and endings of our stories and see how the writing process affects them. No matter how well we construct our plots, we always have a tendency to begin before the beginning and end after the ending. I think that this is because writing takes place on

several levels. Externally, we are tapping at the word processor or moving a pen on paper. In our heads we are constructing sentences and running mental spelling checks. But there is also a deep inner movement that comes to the fore as the story takes over and we begin to live it in the telling. Once we get down to that deep inner journey, the story seems almost to write itself. But in the process of getting to that stage we can write material that will not be part of the final story. Rather, it is a part of the warming-up stage. When you are editing, check your first few paragraphs and see where your story really does begin. In the same way, it can take us a little while to wind down when the story is finished. We come to the end but tend to keep on writing. Find out where the true ending of your story is.

We've looked at the pacing of plot and at beginnings and endings. Let us now look at credibility. A plot must follow logical development, even if the story is fantasy. Only weak plots rely on coincidence. There should be a sort of inevitability about the development of the story as it moves from one stage to another. Are our plots believable? Inexorable? Do they work like well-oiled machines?

Developing a plot

It's all very well to talk about ideals, but how do we develop a good plot?

We come back to our seven- and eight-year-old authors who have a problem that I, as an adult, used to share. I would hear something, see something, and suddenly wheels would spin, bells would ring and I would have a great idea for a story. I'd rush for a pen or typewriter and make a start. But after a bold beginning, the bells would stop ringing and the wheels would seize up. A few sentences and I would be frozen. Most young authors have had this experience. They get a great idea, start writing and stop after two or three sentences.

So, what is the problem? Simply this — we confuse an idea with a plot. An idea is not a plot. It is the seed of a plot and it needs a lot of nurturing, a significant amount of growth, before it can be usefully employed.

My own technique for helping an idea to grow is to keep playing with it, examining possibilities, asking questions, looking for characters. Any character we use is bound to be an extension of ourselves with disguises added. The only characters who come entirely from outside ourselves are the ones who aren't real. If you have written a believable character, you can be sure he or she or it is autobiographical.

Once you establish your characters, the plot will develop in leaps and bounds, quite naturally. If you find that your plot is not developing as it should, back up a little. You may have the wrong character or be asking the wrong questions. Consider options. Try some lateral thinking and a different approach. Or maybe you are just tired. Take a day off, have an early night, and come back to offer your writing peak energy.

For shorter works, I tend to do all the plot development in my head. It sits there, growing like some cerebral pregnancy until it gets to the stage where I can't hold it any longer. It must be born. That is the time for writing it down. But by then, I know the characters so well that if they knocked on the door, I would invite them in for coffee, and the development of the story is complete to the ending.

Some authors prefer to develop their plots with notes and character description on paper. Others, like me, do short stories in their heads. Choose the method that suits you best.

Now, what happens if I have a nice little idea for a story and I know that it is not going to be an earth-shaker? The idea is slow and gentle. It's not dramatic stuff. Not much happens. In other words, I have a soft and unexceptional plot. But I still want to write this story. What do I do? I develop strong and unique characters. I make my characters come alive on the page and dance. And how do I do that? With detail! Not long passages of description that will slow my story, but individual actions and dialogue. I reach out tenaciously and engage my reader through my characters.

So far, I have been talking mainly about shorter works — stories and picture books. Let's give some attention now to the longer work — non-fiction and novels. For both fact and fiction we have much the same concerns: effective arrangement of material, dramatic movement, the rise and fall of events.

With shorter works we are usually concerned with one plot. It is simple and linear, to fit the disciplines of limited space. In the full-length work our major plot often has other dramatic happenings or plots weaving in and out, and these minor plots all affect each other and the main plot, and all help the story to progress. Needless to say, full-length books are not usually planned in one's head, but sketched out on paper first.

I can't remember reading a novel that wasn't in chapter form. There is no reason, from the reader's point of view, why a full-length work should be broken down into chapters. Obviously the convention was invented by the authors to help them plan a book, and I'm sure it's no coincidence that chapters are about short-story length — each a manageable size — and that chapters usually have short-story shape — beginning, middle and ending — within the larger context.

With a full-length work it is essential to know the characters very well before making a start. To some extent these characters will dictate the action. Some of the events that we had intellectually planned for our plot get changed by our characters who refuse to obey our commands. When we know our characters, how they talk, eat, sleep, think, then we put them into situations to see how they react. As always, the most important part of the writing takes place before we get near writing the story — in our head.

When I plan a novel, the main plot comes first. Then one, two or three sub-plots suggest themselves. As I continue to plan the work, I see how the overall action has a natural rise and fall of time and movement that can be divided into chapters. As all this develops, the work will suggest the best way of presenting itself. Will the viewpoint be through one person? If yes, will it be told in the first person? Or third person? Will I have the reader see through the eyes of several characters? Or will there be an eye-of-God view over everything? Each method has its advantages and its restrictions.

Finally, I would like to share with you the process I go through with each work, whether it be a short story, novel or picture book.

This thing called plot

1. I have an idea for a story. I test it. Is it a strong original idea? Worth keeping?

2. I seek solitude and time to develop the idea.

3. What will be the final form of this idea? Early reader? Picture book? Early chapter book? Middle-grade fiction? Adult short story? Novel? The idea itself will suggest the age of the reader and its final form.

4. I expand the idea by asking questions of it. I keep turning it in my mind. A neglected idea will go cold.

5. At each stage of development I test the idea against real life, especially against my childhood and the children I know, to see if it sounds authentic. I look for detail that is going to make my story fresh and original. I realise that it is detail that gives life to the story.

6. I build the backbone of the story first — the plot. Everything else in the story will hang from this spine.

7. When the storyline is so real to me that it has a life of its own, I start writing. I write freely, totally absorbed in giving birth to the story within me.

8. I edit, trimming away material that does not further the plot and perhaps adding where impact is lacking. I ask myself, 'What actually happens in this story?' I even ask the brutal question, 'Is there a good reason why this story should exist?' 'What is new/unique about this story that warrants publication?'

9. I look with an editorial eye at beginnings and endings. Does my reader have to wade through unnecessary introduction to get to my story? Are my characters living and breathing, or flat and faceless? What detail have I used to make them come alive and express their individuality? How do I deal with the main crunch point in the story? Do I pass over it or

do I give it value? How do I pace the story? After all, a story should be like music with loud and soft, fast and quiet passages. What 'voice' have I used to tell this story?

10. No matter how eager I am to display my new creation, I put the work away for a week or even a month before I do the final editing. I need that space to disconnect myself emotionally from the story. Once I have 'fallen out of love' with it, my critical sense is sharpened and I can evaluate the work objectively. I pay particular attention to beginnings and endings. Do my first sentences grab the reader?

11. I send the story out to stand on its own feet in a world busy with stories, and I avoid eye contact with the mailbox by immersing myself in another work.

2. DIALOGUE

You probably realise that most writing topics lean against each other. We can't separate plot from character. Nor is it possible to talk about character without mentioning dialogue. Dialogue grows from character.

We have all read stories in which the dialogue has been interchangeable. The characters have all used the same way of speaking, the same word patterns, the same responses to questions, the same exclamations. If you took away the 'he said' and 'she said' you wouldn't know who was talking. That kind of dialogue comes to us automatically. It is what I call 'information dialogue'. We know that our characters are going to have a certain spoken exchange and this is the information that is going to be in this exchange. It is all there, lying on top of our thinking. We write it down without reflecting too much about the way we are presenting it. Our characters are simply mouthpieces for our words.

Then we read dialogue that makes a character leap from a page. The words don't just convey information. They portray the life of the speaker with stunning colour and accuracy.

How can we write dialogue like that? How can we make our

characters come alive to our readers? I offer some awareness exercises that have helped me.

1. Develop an ear for dialogue

It sounds simple and obvious but actually, we usually listen for information. We don't listen with awareness. Become a student of conversation. Eavesdrop on planes and buses. Listen to talkback shows. Tune in not so much for information as to discover how people put words together. Take notes. Listen for repetition, rhythm, sentence formation, pacing, pauses, areas where the voice is strong or areas where it is weak.

The first thing you will notice is that people rarely speak in prose. Convincing dialogue is not made up from tidy prose — subject, verb, object, subject, verb, object. Speech is a free expression of character and it does not obey the strict rules of narrative or grammar. This is wonderful for a writer. It is so freeing.

The second thing we discover is that people do not always say exactly what they mean. There is often an important sub-text that reveals a lot about the speaker. One woman says, 'I have just found this most amazing little dress shop. You have to go there.' Sub-text: please compliment me on my appearance. The second woman responds, 'I'd love to but I'm going to be so busy!' Sub-text: I have a weight problem and they wouldn't have my size.

Have you noticed that when people say, 'By the way' they are coming to the main point of their part of the conversation? It is never by the way. It is always important.

When we become dedicated students of dialogue, we discover that everyone has an accent — everyone. There is a general accent that says something about country, region and perhaps, education. Then there are specific inflections that tell us something about the age and personality of the speaker. People have repetitive phrases or inflections: 'You know what I mean? So I went, you know, right in there and I told him. You know? I told him straight to his face and he just looked at me, he did. Just looked. You know? And not a word.'

We also realise that speech structure changes according to the speaker's physical and emotional state. We can detect when people are tired or angry, sick or scared. We know from the speech patterns when people are breathless or intoxicated or very excited about something. Much depends on who the person is speaking to, and the relationship involved. Sentence structures change subtly when people are trying to impress or are romantically impressed, when they are lying, trying to hide something.

Eventually, we come to the realisation that speech patterns are as individual as fingerprints, and that no two people are exactly alike in the way they communicate with others.

2. Awareness of human uniqueness is our starting point in writing good dialogue

This means that we must be aware of the uniqueness of our character. If we don't have that awareness, then we need to work on the characters until they are so real to us that we would recognise them anywhere.

We need to remember that characters are not usually born with this uniqueness. Quite often characters arrive in our heads simply as furniture for a story. We don't know a lot about them. We don't care a lot about them. Or sometimes the character slips in quietly from some childhood trauma from our past. We don't recognise where this character has come from, but we recognise that he or she is lonely and we feel sorry for him or her. Beware of that character who makes you feel pity. Empathy, yes. Sympathy, no. If you are telling your reader that he or she has to feel sorry for your character, the reader will want to drown that character. Readers do not like to be told what to think.

Remember that the mind works immediately on well-worn paths. This means your first reaction in almost any situation will be a cliché. The first aspects of character and dialogue that come to an author will be stereotypes and clichés. We have to work past the clichés. We have to push back the boundaries. This means consciously working on our characters to develop their uniqueness. It is a genesis project. We form them from the rough clay of the cliché and then we breathe individuality into them and we go on breathing into them until they are fully alive and unique in every detail. And when we know everything about them, we also know how they will speak and interact with each other.

Well, here we are with our characters fully alive, their voices in our heads, ready to go. But there is more to it than that. How do we use dialogue as part of the engineering in our story?

3. We can be aware of what dialogue does to the pacing of a plot

Dialogue tends to quicken plot. It breaks up large chunks of narrative that can get rather heavy for a young reader — or an older one, for that matter. For this reason I use speech even if my character is in a solitary situation. A spoken monologue or internal speech, a character having a mental conversation with himself, is useful for changing the pace of text on the page. We all know that our eyes become restless if they are confronted with too much solid narrative. We can lose focus and start skipping over the pages, looking for action, looking

for a break in the pattern, looking for dialogue. Many children give up on a book saying, 'There isn't enough talking in it.' We are social animals. For some deeply atavistic reason, we need dialogue in our reading.

4. Dialogue can also be a wonderful, economical way of pushing our plot

Sometimes a few spoken words can carry our characters and action further than half a page of description. This occurs especially when we layer meaning, when the words that our characters use carry a sub-text that connects with the reader. This is always a powerful way of advancing plot because it demands a commitment from the reader. We are not explaining the story away. We are dealing with innuendo that must be decoded. We know from our own experience that some of the funniest comedy or the most potent tragedy is portrayed in dialogue sub-text. Action is the right accompaniment to speech, not passive observation. By this, I mean verbs, not adverbs. Avoid qualifying speech with adverbs like, 'he said sleepily' or 'she said sarcastically' or 'he muttered bravely'. The speech itself should give the context. But action involving body language can help, especially when there is a sub-text. For example:

'No, honest!' He rubbed his nose. 'I really, really like it.'

Or something like this:

Dad picked the cat hair off the cushion and rolled it between his fingers. 'Not long, son. Just until your mother and I sort out a few things.'

Always remember what your character is doing while he or she is speaking.

5. Dialogue is a reliable way to grab your readers' attention

If you are struggling for an interesting beginning to a story, try opening with dialogue. If you have a long piece of narrative that sits heavily on the page and the reader, break it with dialogue. Not just any dialogue. Remember what we said about the uniqueness of characters? Your dialogue needs to be highly individual and to have layers of meaning.

Read the writers of good dialogue and see your favourite movies a second and even a third time, to analyse the dialogue. You will be amazed at how much is said in very few words.

3. DISCIPLINE

Some people still hold the view that writing is a form of self-indulgence. It is supposed to be something we do when the mood or muse takes us. People have seriously asked me, 'Are you writing or are you working?'

Writing demands more discipline than any profession I know. If you are going to train in any of the other arts, you will have a teacher to instruct you and set goals for you. Your personal discipline will be assisted by guidelines perhaps enforced by that teacher standing over you. The art or music student, the dancer, the actor, the singer, all have supervised training.

The writer is alone. Certainly there are other writers who can share their experience. There are editors who can offer valuable technical assistance. There are families and friends who will be supportive. There are books and workshops that can inspire. But essentially the writer must find her or his own way. The writer is responsible for self-instruction and self-discipline.

No writer can tell another writer how to write. But there are experiences which most of us share and certain truths that apply to us all. What I am going to offer you is a list resembling a collection of handy household hints. You will probably have notes to add to the list.

The view of writing as self-indulgence is even held by some people who are feeling the urge to take up writing. I've had people tell me I'm lucky because I have so much inspiration. I don't know how to answer that. Then again, some think that to be a writer means waiting for ideal conditions and a large chunk of time. I can't count how often someone has told me about the book they're going to write when they retire. The truth is that inspiration does not fall like rain on some and not others. We have to seek it. Time for writing doesn't just happen. We make it. And if we could find those ideal conditions for writing, we probably wouldn't write, because our work comes from the stuff of life. We write well under some pressure. We do not write well in a vacuum. If we could remove ourselves from everyday living, then we would find ourselves divorced from the source of our art.

When looking at discipline, we could do well to start by looking at our writing conditions.

1. Time

Unless we are embarking on another *War and Peace* our writing can be accomplished quite comfortably within a day involving other work and other people. The important thing is to make and keep a regular block of time. One hour at the same time every day is better than, say, a whole day once a week, because the work is kept alive within you from day to day. You live with your story. Your mind is doing things with it, even while you are occupied with other work. But if you write on only one day of the week, no matter that you have given eight hours to it, your story will go cold during the week when you are waiting for your writing day to come round again.

2. Peak energy

Let's say that you have arranged your time so that you have one or two hours a day for your writing. Where in the day do you place those two hours? At your peak energy time! Now, this is very important. Creative work comes from the top 25 percent of our energy, and we need to give writing our best. I am convinced that what people call writers' block is actually flat batteries. If we try to work on flagging energy then inspiration won't come. I'll repeat this because it is vital to our productivity: creative thinking, inspiration — genius, if you like — comes from peak energy. So, if you are a morning person, try writing between 5.00 and 7.00 a.m. If you sparkle in the evenings, you might like to shut yourself away between 8.00 and 10.00 p.m. Tell everyone that you cannot be interrupted during this time: no family, no phone, no distractions of any kind.

Beware of the distractions you offer yourself. There will be times when you are tempted to make a fourth cup of coffee or to clean your desk or call someone on the phone, or walk round like a caged bear. Sit in that chair in front of that pad, computer, word processor, whatever you use, and stay there for the whole two hours. If you don't write anything the time isn't wasted. You are training yourself to focus. And you will eventually start writing.

3. Place

Try to find a place free from distractions, comfortable but not too comfortable, warm but not too warm. You need to feel alert in this place. It's best if you have a place where your work can remain set up. For more than 20 years I typed on a kitchen table that had to be cleared after every writing session. That was a nuisance, as was setting up again each time. The place of work should not change. Some writers say that they can work anywhere. Those are writers who are very skilled in self-discipline. Most of us need to form habits of place and time. When our surroundings are so familiar that we are not aware of them, then we are less likely to be distracted and more easily able to move into that inner space where our story is.

Again, protect your work space from intrusion. No phone in the room. No visitors bearing questions. Remember that writing demands solitude. It also thrives on set routine.

Coming away from a writing session is a bit like coming out of an anaesthetic. Your mind needs a little time to adjust to the world out there. If you are an early morning writer, you can try a brisk ten-minute walk. Night owls can sleep.

4. Work methods

We usually set up our own work methods according to personal preferences and the patterns we have established. Some writers will write and revise a novel right through, from beginning to end with each draft. Others will write and revise one chapter at a time. Some prefer to do a first draft in longhand. Some work from a visual approach. They see the story acted out in their imagination and record what they see. Others are aural. They hear words and take down dictation. Still others work from a visual and aural combination. As writers, we have different strengths. One will excel at dialogue, another will be best at narrative. Some will think readily in rhythm and rhyme, others

have the gift of humour. Work methods and writing styles are as individual as fingerprints.

However, we can set up certain disciplines that will help our unique creativity. It is helpful if we can set ourselves realistic goals and work towards them. We should allow ourselves plenty of time for each project so that we can make unhurried revisions. Within the time-span for each project, we can make lists or timetables. For example, a week's plan could look like this: Monday, Tuesday, Wednesday, first draft of Chapter Three. Thursday and Friday, second draft of Chapter Three.

By setting goals, making lists and/or timetables, we place a structure over a largely abstract process and make it tangible. Our work becomes visible to us as something that we control and manage, not something that happens by chance. This feeling of being in control is helpful to the image of ourselves as disciplined writers. It also aids our productivity.

5. Planning

We need to plan our work. Many of us get an idea and start writing, without first making plans. We would not build a house without plans, simply because we had the materials. Nor would we cut into a length of silk without knowing what the finished garment was going to look like. Yet we do this with our writing.

How we plan a work largely depends on its length. Much of a short story or picture book can be planned in the head with a few notes on paper. A longer work will require more extensive and detailed notes.

I have a planning folder for each novel I write. In it, I have the clippings and notes that are a part of the research for the work. A book that featured a draught horse? There is a leaflet about the horse's ailments, a picture of the muscle and bone structure of a Clydesdale horse, an old picture of some Clydesdales pulling a plough. There are notes about the other characters — their dates of birth, appearance, personality, hobbies, likes and dislikes, etc. I have drawn a map of a farm and house, another map of the

farm in relation to the nearest town and highway. Then there is
a one-page outline of the story, plus a chapter breakdown. The
novel eventually became *Bow Down Shadrach*.

You may work to a different method. The important thing is
to have a plan.

6. Inspiration

But what if you don't have an idea for a story? How do you
'plan' inspiration?

I've mentioned that inspiration doesn't usually come without
invitation. We have to seek it. To receive it and do something
with it, we also need lots of good energy.

The world is stuffed full of things to write about. Inspiration
is largely a matter of selection, of seeing, hearing, sifting what
is around us and being aware of the way it resonates with our
own experience. Ideas for stories come daily. We can fail to
notice them. Or we can notice them and then forget them.

There is an old Hebrew belief that we notice what we are
meant to notice. I carry with me a notebook in which I jot
down anything that makes a statement to me. It might be an
interesting name, or an intriguing exchange in conversation.
It might be a description of something seen, or one of those
odd fragments that come into the mind seemingly from
nowhere. One double page from my notebook has the
following notes:

1. Boondoggle. Nice-sounding word. A story with a
   Dr Boondoggle?

2. Nine-year-old girl talking about sickness at school.
   'No one in our school is healthy. I tell you, if you saw
   a healthy kid at our school, there'd be something
   wrong with her.'

3. The giant with the big boots: 'So he put on his
   clod-hoppers and marched over the dingle-bells.'

4. Mrs T.M. puts mouse traps on her furniture to keep
   the dogs off it.

5. Pigeon Princess. Once there was a princess who lived in a high tower. She knew it was a high tower because the cars below were as big as grasshoppers, and she knew she was a princess because that's what her grandmother called her.
'Princess, you been feeding those pigeons again?'

Every now and then I pick up my notebook and thumb through it. Most of the notes will be dead and have no meaning for me, but some will send out the green shoots of ideas that in turn will grow into stories.

A writer is constantly fishing for inspiration.

7. Editorial discipline

A publisher suggested to me that the difference between the amateur writer and the professional was that the professional enjoyed editing his or her own work. I pondered on this and thought it probably true to some extent. When I began writing for publication, it never occurred to me that I should rewrite stories. Over the space of a couple of years I sent 49 short stories to the same magazine and had them all returned. I didn't get a story published until I had learned the hard lesson that no story is born perfect. Or, to use another metaphor, we all produce rough diamonds which require many hours of cutting and polishing to become commercial property.

When I began writing, I did not enjoy editing, mainly because I didn't know how. I am not sure that I know much more now, but I do rewrite a story from five to ten times, and yes, I get pleasure from the craft side of writing.

What are some of the hints to be passed on?

The first is the recognition that all work needs editing. New writers can feel possessive of their work and sensitive to criticism. It is true that a story is a part of us, but when we write it for publication we are making a gift of it to a reader and we have to consider the needs of that reader.

The second is the recognition that it takes a little time for us to see our work objectively. While the story is still alive within us, our editorial vision is to some extent clouded. If you can, revise your manuscript to the best of your ability and then put it away for a week or two while you get on with other writing. When you are totally involved with something else, you will be able to take out the manuscript and clearly see what you have written.

Editing tips are in chapter 10, Putting on your Editor's Hat. Here it is sufficient to say that a disciplined approach to editing is greatly rewarding both in satisfaction and effect.

8. Presentation

Our story or novel is as good as we can possibly make it, and now it is time to send it out. We need to be professional in our presentation. A publisher or commissioning editor is going to have a mountain of manuscripts on her desk. Chances are she will not look at my manuscript if it is crumpled or untidy or poorly set out or printed in faint ink. (See chapter 11, Presentation, for more on this subject.)

Make sure you are sending your work to an appropriate publisher. Know the kind of material a house publishes. Look at their catalogue. Does your work fit?

If you have a novel, don't send it to a publisher until they ask to see it. Send first a one-page summary of the novel plus a copy of the first chapter.

I now have an agent who submits work for me but until recently I used to send out my own stories. Because some publishers can keep a manuscript a year or more before making a decision, I found it easier to give them and me, a time limit. I would state politely in my covering letter that they had three months in which to consider this manuscript and at the end of that time I would be submitting it to another publisher. If the publisher wanted it, they'd contact me almost immediately. Sometimes I didn't get a reply at all, but that didn't matter. I knew that by a certain date I was free to send the story elsewhere.

Always put a copyright notice on your manuscript, and send a stamped addressed envelope for return mailing.

Your manuscript has now been mailed. Don't hang about in limbo, waiting to see what happens. Get on with the next work.

Oh-oh! So you have got a rejection slip. Join the club. We all get rejection slips. And I don't mean past tense. I still get stories rejected. So do other veteran writers.

There are all sort of reasons why a story is returned, so don't take it as personal rejection. You've sent in a funny Christmas story and this week the publisher has received ten funny Christmas stories. You've written a novel about a ten-year-old girl in France during World War II. Well, last year they published a great book with a similar plot. The most common reason for returning a work is that there are other stories like it, already published. That's something to remember.

9. Support

Some of us claim that we write for ourselves. I don't think that is true. Writing is all about communication, and it's a form of communication that must be executed in solitude. We need feedback. We need support. To some extent we find support from our immediate clan — family and friends — but it is also important to be in contact with other writers who speak and understand the same professional language.

If you do not have a writers' group in your area, consider starting one. An advertisement in a local newspaper or library is usually enough to get a regular gathering of writers established. Most writers' groups meet to read and critique manuscripts and share writing/editing/publishing experience. While it can be helpful to read work to others, I would caution you about talking out stories that have not yet been written. All too often, the energy of a story is dissipated by talk and is not there when you sit down to write it.

10. Know what is out there

I'm always surprised at the number of writers who don't read the works of others. If you are going to sell your work, you need to know what is being published, who published it and who is reading it. Talk to children about their favourite books. Find out why they like them. Ask them about the books they don't like. Be aware of what works for different ages. Every now and then, spend a couple of hours in a children's library, look at books and chat to librarians. You'll find the time well spent.

11. Go for it!

This list of suggestions seems formidable. It hints of a journey full of great difficulty and danger, and I don't want to give that impression. Writing does need a lot of discipline if it's to go anywhere, but none of it is arduous. It is all personally enriching and deeply satisfying. I find writing hard work but at the same time consider myself greatly blessed in that my work is also my greatest pleasure.

4. HUMOUR

Humour is never taken seriously. True! There is huge potential for research into humour, its reflection in art and literature, and, most importantly, its effect. Why do we seek humour? Why do we need to laugh?

The obvious answer is that laughter relieves tension. We know how relaxed we feel after a good comedy show. Not only relaxed; somehow, laughter has restored objectivity. The sea of problems that threatened to drown us has become distant, a small puddle. We go to bed and sleep well, with laughter still rising in us like champagne bubbles.

Well, that's us, the big people. What about children? How does humour cater for their needs?

For the very young child, laughter is the natural reaction to a feeling of well-being. Talk to a four-month-old baby and watch its face crease into a smile, hear the smile gurgle into laughter. Play peek-a-boo! with a one-year-old, and watch the excitement resolve itself in laughter. Games, jokes, funny faces, silly noises, are all food and drink to the toddler. By five, the child is actively looking for jokes and wanting to tell them. No matter how many times a young child tells a joke, he or she will usually laugh loudly with the telling. Jokes are very important to early education. Laughter is an atavistic need.

As authors of books for children, how do we meet this need? First, we are going to talk about the functions of humour in a book for young readers. Then we'll look at the kind of humour we write, and why.

Release through laughter

Let's look at the physiological function of laughter — the release of tension. I became aware of this back in the late 1960s when I started writing for reluctant readers. I was the mother of four young children, writing short stories for adults. I had also completed my first novel for adults. My elder son Edward, a very practical little boy, was not interested in reading. He was sandwiched between sisters who could both read before they started school, and he was not going to compete. He liked engines, building things, making models. At seven, his attitude to reading was negative. With his teacher's encouragement, I wrote stories for him and about him. Hero stories. Later, I worked in the same way with other children in that school, and then neighbouring schools. That was how I became committed to writing for reluctant readers.

My writing was shaped by the children with whom I worked. They taught me many valuable lessons. The most important lesson was this: a child cannot be tense while he or she is laughing.

Back in the 1960s, dyslexia was a popular diagnosis. Many of the children I worked with had been arbitrarily labelled 'dyslexic' because they did mirror writing, but I noticed that they had no right/left directional confusion in those activities they enjoyed. They had good ball-handling skills, could make intricate models, do puzzles like jigsaws, and use scissors, a stapler, a screwdriver, hammer and nails, or a slingshot — all with accuracy. No fumbling. I concluded that their problem with reading came down to tension through fear of failure. All had a negative image of themselves as readers and this was portrayed in their body language as soon as a school reading book was produced. It was so rewarding to see that tension disappear in laughter. The surprise of a joke in a story was like scissors on taut elastic. Instant release.

The distancing effect of laughter

For children as well as adults, humour helps objectivity by distancing us from our serious concerns. For the young people who taught me how to write for them, the serious concern was the act of attempting to read. Books were the enemy. Suddenly, though, a book could become a friend. It was no longer boring. It was no longer something to be feared. It was funny. It had meaning.

The affirming effect of laughter

Here's another thing about humour. It not only relaxes us, enhancing objectivity, it also nourishes the ego. In some subtle way, it makes us feel good about ourselves. I suspect this is because a joke demands a response from us. We have to make a connection in order to find the joke. In making that connection, we not only find laughter, we also feel successful. A joke empowers us because it puts us in a superior position.

This seems to be doubly so for children. Funny stories increase the child's self-esteem.

The balancing effect of laughter

Humour enables us to deal safely with the more serious aspects of life.

Life is a balance of light and shade, laughter and tears. It seems that the bleaker the situation, the greater our need for laughter. How many of us know the nervous giggle at a moment of tension? Why is it that funny things seem to happen at funerals?

In 1968, at a time of significant loss, I had about six months of quite severe depression. As I recovered, I found I did not want sympathy. I did not want medication or counselling or anything that seemed like a scab-picking exercise. I wanted to laugh. I gravitated towards humorous films, funny friends, looked for jokes and cartoons. I guess I was not light company myself, but I craved laughter the way a sick dog will eat grass. Humour was the emetic for depression.

How does that apply to us as authors? If we are writing about a serious subject, we need balance and humour. We read many serious 'message' books that are devoid of humour. Why? For a moment, look back at the books we loved when we were children. How was the serious message of fidelity and steadfastness dealt with in *Horton the Elephant*? How does Arnold Lobel of *Frog and Toad* fame deal with the heavy childhood issues of fear, embarrassment, illness?

What kind of humour appeals to young readers?

First of all, and this is important, we should write situation humour. We do not put people down. We do not make jokes at people's expense, certainly never at a child's expense. We laugh with our characters, not at them.

Next, we need to be aware of the age for which we are writing and shape the humour to suit. Pre-school children often have a fondness for slapstick humour. They have a growing awareness of their bodies and are interested in bottoms, fingers, toes, belly-buttons. Mouths are for attempts at whistling, noses are for sniffing good smells and bad, eyes are for winking and crossing in the mirror. Ears get in the way of haircuts, haircuts make your back itchy, a back is something to scratch on the door frame. Except Dad's back! That's something to ride like a horse. Many of Arnold Lobel's funny stories, like 'Tear-water tea' in the book *Owl at Home*, are based on the young child's awareness of body.

Children in the first years of school enjoy double meanings, puns, word games, jokes based on misunderstanding or accidents of coincidence. They are looking for more sophisticated jokes, humour that demands more from the reader. They also like situation humour, which often happens

with the juxtaposition of the ordinary and the ludicrous. It can occur when you take a different slant on a familiar theme.

There is a kind of humour that openly flatters the young reader. Remember when you were seven? You were perhaps a bit shy. Your skills in most areas were undeveloped and life was full of learning moments. No doubt there were a few big people around to let you know when you made a mistake. So wasn't it a relief to see a two- or three-year-old make the kind of mistakes that you had grown out of? In books, children enjoy stories about characters who act like younger siblings and that, again, is the appeal of writers like Dr Seuss and Arnold Lobel.

Humour can be carried in your choice of words, through rich and inventive language. Consider the genius of Margaret Mahy in using original language structures to bring laughter to the child.

Many children's picture books are serious in a kindly, gloomy way, and there are young adult novels that offer sympathy in the context of bleakness. There is an earnest attempt on the part of the author to relate to the child out there who is suffering. Well, when we observe children in bad situations, we see that humour is never very far away. They tend to freeze when threatened, and then thaw when someone turns on the light of laughter. As for young adults, the teen years are times of great emotional highs and lows. Does a depressed young person need a book that says, you poor thing, how you suffer, but I will show you the light at the end of the tunnel? No. I don't think so.

So why do we encounter so many humourless books? I believe it's because when we write, we go on a deep interior journey and the first emotions to come up will be sad ones. This is because fear is the most potent of our emotions. It has to be. It is connected directly to the instinct for survival and it keeps us safe. Young children know quite a lot of fear. These days we talk about insecurity, but actually it's plain old-fashioned fear: fear of being alone, fear of strange places, fear of failure, embarrassment, inadequacy, bullies, dreams that became nightmares. These emotions get bottled up and many years later they come out in what I call 'therapy writing'. This is something that happens to us all. It's good that we write this stuff. But it belongs in journal writing, not in children's books, because it's written not to rescue the child out there but the child within us.

If we feel sympathy for the young character in the story we are writing, that should ring an alarm bell. We feel empathy for characters, not sympathy. Life is always a balance of light and shade. The good news is that once we have written out this therapy stuff, the humour comes up like a clear bubbling spring.

I can raise areas of awareness. I can talk to you about the importance of humour. But I can't tell you what to write. You will have that knowledge within you when you speak to your own inner child. Remember that your childhood is not behind you. It is within you. Whenever you need resource material for your writing, you can access this library of experience.

What made us laugh when we were children?

There are the universal situations that transcend cultures — humour associated with weather or geographical features or inanimate objects. We can all relate to jokes about cars that break down or washing machines that flood the house with suds. We understand funny stories about being stuck in mud, or rolling down a hill, or having an umbrella blow inside out. We've been there. Our inner child knows what it's like.

Then there is situation humour, arising from relationship — family connections, emotional reactions and misunderstandings. Most TV comedy is based on situation humour, but we need to remember always that we are writing about the child's world, the child's aspiration and values — not ours. We all see from time to time those picture books where the humour is at the child's expense. I do not advocate that kind of writing.

Sometimes, fantasy will advance humour in a way that reality cannot. *Mrs Wishy Washy* works as a story about a scrub-happy woman farmer and three animals. It would not work with a mother and three children, which is after all what the story is about. If you are using anthropomorphism (i.e. talking animals), try to have your animals acting true to their nature. Editors have a problem with anthropomorphism when the animals are in human dress, behaving like humans.

Humour requires crisp, vibrant language. Play with words. Be aware that they are the tools of your comedy. So are the gaps between them. Often what you don't say is as funny as what you say. But as your own editor, learn to be ruthless when pruning language. Funny stories demand a cracking pace.

Whether you are writing a deliberately funny story or poem, or whether you are threading in humour to lighten a more serious work, good humour tends to fulfil the author as much as the reader. That's the test. Do you sit at the computer, gazing at the screen, laughter rising from your inner child, to your adult eyes and mouth? Good. That means it will work for your reader.

5. WRITING FOR THE NEW READER

This is probably the most difficult level, although it appears simple. Children learning to read need to see themselves as successful long before they are, in fact, fluent readers.

They need a real story that is interesting, entertaining, educationally and emotionally supportive, a story that is child-centred. An effective early reading book has a real story, and if word repetition is used, it cannot be static. It must drive the plot. The text does not talk down to the reader. It respects the reader's authority and intelligence but at the same is simple and accessible. The story has real plot development, a beginning, a middle and a satisfying ending. Although much of the story can be told in the illustrations, the story must make sense when read on its own, without pictures.

Here are some suggestions for rectifying common misunderstandings of what is required in an early reading book.

A real story is important, but choose a simple plot. The story can be based on a joke or a childhood memory. The plot can have a simple cause/effect structure. Remember that it needs to be appropriate for the age of the reader.

It is a mistake to write 'message' stories because these usually come from an adult perception of what a child needs. Most stories contain messages but the message is not the reason for the writing.

If you are using anthropomorphism, make sure that the animals behave like animals and are not dressed like people and in human roles.

Avoid word repetition that is not a natural part of the story. Too many early reading books read like shopping lists.

If you want to know the level or degree of challenge of your

story, count the range of words. I've seen stories of 50 words that are more difficult than Dr Seuss's *Green Eggs and Ham*, which has over 1000 words. When you have worked out the word range, cross out the words that will be illustrated. When a child meets a new word, s/he looks to the picture for clues. The words that can't be illustrated — was, there, us, them, said, should, and so on — are known as service words. These are the words that are learned by context and use, and too many can create an obstacle to success for the emergent reader.

Don't forget the value of humour. Children love jokes, and laughter has a way of dissolving a tense attitude to reading.

Don't illustrate your early reading story. Publishers have their own illustrators and rarely accept an illustrated work. But most publishers are happy for you to make a note regarding an illustration, where necessary.

The shaping of an early reading story is usually done by a professional who has years of specialised experience. You may, however, wish to know why the story that you have written is changed. Here are the reasons.

Simplification

The world is full of material for competent young readers. It is the beginner reader who concerns us. We try to simplify the story to make the degree of challenge meaningful and manageable.

Many editors will work with a table of the words most frequently used by children.

At an early level there will be an emphasis on decodable words — words that sound like their spelling.

A distinction is made between those 'interest' words that will have clues in the pictures, and the 'service' words that cannot be illustrated.

The editor will have some idea of the reading level of the finished story and will edit according to that level, repeating the service words for reinforcement, and avoiding the juxtaposition of words that could be confusing in the same sentence — for example, 'there' and 'their', or 'was' and 'saw'.

There will be an awareness of line breaks (see section on line breaks later in this chapter) and text may be changed to facilitate an appropriate line break and/or line length.

There will also be awareness of sentence structure, the complexity of which depends on the reading level.

Editing for illustration

At an early reading level, much of the story is told in the pictures with a supporting text. With this in mind, the editor may need to make textual change for the following reasons.

There may be two actions in a short paragraph and only one can be illustrated.

Adjectives that can be illustrated are usually removed from the text.

There needs to be a page-to-page story progression in the pictures as well as the text. Repetition of illustration can be boring and needs to be avoided.

The story needs a well-defined beginning/middle/ending in illustration as well as text. The words on each page will facilitate this.

Vocabulary

If you have written a story for early reading, try the following test. Put a ring around every word that can be shown in an illustration. Now work out the range of words you have left. That will give you an indication of reading challenge.

With this test, my book *Mrs Wishy-Washy* has a vocab range of about 25 words even though it is a fully formed story. The editor will be concerned with managing the vocabulary range for the level.

Dialogue

Children like 'talking' in their books and an editor will try to achieve a balance between dialogue and narrative.

Syntax

The editor will introduce the appropriate arrangement of words, sentence structures and punctuation for the level.

Child-centred art

Illustration styles vary, and although it is good that children be exposed to variety, it is important that the artwork be child-friendly. This is especially so for the emergent reader.

Avoid exaggeration and distortion. Children tend to be literal in interpretation. A cartoon style of illustration can be fun, but young readers do not like excessive distortion, especially of faces. They can see big eyes as fierce and big mouths as menacing.

There is a preference for strong bright colour, although some books with black and white illustrations are popular.

Young children connect with what they see. Thus, a giant illustrated from the waist down can be interpreted as half a giant, or part of a house in the background can be seen as a 'broken house'. Objects should be shown in entirety at this early level of reading.

Children need to see faces. They feel uneasy about pictures showing the backs of heads. Children also dislike pictures of people laughing with eyes wide open. When we smile or laugh, our eyes tend to close a little. A laughing mouth and wide-open eyes is seen as a threatening grimace.

Illustration for meaning

The author and illustrator are both bound by the fact that the book is for children learning to read. The pictures should contain nothing more and nothing less than is required by the text. The illustrator has the responsibility for providing picture clues for the words.

Placement of characters

The illustrator needs to introduce characters in art in the same order that they appear in the text. If the text says 'a frog and a duck' and the illustrator depicts a duck to the left of the page and a frog to the right, then the wrong picture clues are given. Similarly, if the illustration shows a frog and a duck with a cow in the background, the reader will look for the word 'cow' in the text.

Direction

There needs to be a left-to-right movement throughout the book. Some children come to reading with very little book-handling experience. If they see a car going from right to left in the illustration, they might turn the pages backwards to see where the car is going. It is important at this level that the movement in the illustration is towards the right so that children turn pages in the correct sequence.

Humour

Humour in art is as important as it is in writing. The illustrator can show warm soft humour, or outrageous slapstick, depending on the story. In one of my books, *A Barrel of Gold*, a dog chases and bites the pants of a robber. Illustrator Robyn Belton showed the robber's pants torn, revealing red spotted underwear. That is the favourite page for young readers.

Page layout

Most early reading books have 8, 16 or 24 pages plus a cover. The first page is the title page so this means there are up to 7, 15 or 23 pages of story and illustration. The layout of any book is usually done by the publishing house — the editor and the art director. But it is useful for an author to know the reasons for text placement.

Pagination

The story is broken down into movements like scenes in a film. It is desirable to have one action to a page or double-page spread. The text and imagined pictures should have a momentum that builds the story to a climax. There will be a satisfying resolution on the last page.

The text will sit naturally at the top or bottom of the page, depending on whether the illustration depicts the beginning or end of the text.

The young reader needs to be able to predict the print. Text placement, words used and illustrations done for meaning will all help the reader make accurate predictions, and will increase reading confidence.

Attention is given to the appropriate number of lines to each page. In an early emergent eight-page book, two lines per page, large print, are about right.

A clear print font resembling the print that is familiar to children is desirable. Fancy fonts can increase difficulty. As fluency develops, four to eight lines to a page are usual. A fluent reader has no problem with full pages of text in larger chapter books, but some illustration is still desirable for those in transition between picture books and novels.

Line breaks

Watch a new reader with a book. She or he will usually read aloud, tracking a line of text with a finger. At the end of the line she or he will take a breath and then track back to the next line. Some children take three or four seconds to do this.

It is important that each line can be read easily with one breath, and the break at the end does not destroy meaning. Try reading these lines slowly with a three-second pause at the end of each line, and you will see what I mean.

> *'Oh lovely mud!'*
> *said the cow*
> *and she jumped in it.*

*'Oh lovely mud!' said
the cow and she
jumped in it.*

Title page and cover

In planning a book, I find it is helpful to the reader if I visually set up the story on the cover and then progress it on the title page. The illustration notes for the cover suggest a picture that describes the title and also opens the story. The cover page can then move the story along so that the young reader is engaged with the story before encountering print other than the title.

Any imprint information (containing details such as publisher, date of publication and ISBN number) should be kept to a small unobtrusive font on the inside front cover. Likewise any teacher information needs to be small and unobtrusive on the inside back cover.

6. NOVELS FOR CHILDREN AND YOUNG ADULTS

Many writers consider the novel to be the most difficult area of juvenile fiction. I don't know why.

I get the impression that most writers imagine that the younger the reader and the fewer the words needed, the greater the chance of success. The general view seems to be that fiction for the middle-school years (middle-grade fiction) is easier than upper grades, picture books are easier than middle-grade fiction, and early reading texts are easier than picture books. I see it the other way around.

Writing for the upper grades is the easiest. My background life experience is closer to this age group than the others. At the other end of the scale, a truly successful early reading text is very difficult. There must be a strong idea that can be carried in dynamic, high-interest illustrations, and then that idea must be expressed with a controlled vocabulary in such a way that it appears fresh and interesting. Sometimes it seems to me that writing an early reading text is like inventing a crossword puzzle in which there are no black spaces. Give me the task of a senior chapter book, any day.

If we were to ask a children's trade book publisher — that is, a publisher who does library and bookshop titles — what are the manuscripts you mostly receive, we would be told, picture books and junior chapter books. The thin area is young adult fiction, especially good strong chapter books for adolescents aged 13 to 16. Most publishers will tell you that there is a shortage of material for this age group. For writers looking at markets, it makes sense to aim for the space where there is the least competition.

Starting on fiction

Okay, so let's say that now we have decided to write a work of fiction for adolescents. (I'm dealing with fiction because non-fiction is not my field and I can't talk from ignorance.) So where do we start?

The idea comes first. Something seen, something heard, a situation that connects with us and moves into our creative space. Sometimes two or more ideas will coalesce. The beginnings of *Starbright and the Dreameater* were a fusion of quantum theory and classical messianic stories. *The Silent One* started with first impressions of a Fijian island and a request from a teacher to write something for deaf children. Whatever the inspiration, we know the validity of the idea by its strength. A weak idea will drift away. A strong idea will fill us with passion. So there it is, a good strong idea for a novel, and now we need to develop it.

It is very likely that the idea originated somewhere out there but as long as it stays out there as a head experience, it will not be convincing. It must be internalised. A story that's not real to the author will not be real to young readers.

How do we internalise a story? We connect it to our own experience. In each of us, the adolescent is still alive and authentic. But sometimes it takes a little time and meditation to connect authentically with our adolescent years. As adults, we are often embarrassed or even irritated by our adolescence and we are tempted to rewrite it. Adolescence is a turbulent time, full of exaggerated highs and lows. Looking back, we tend to flatten the mood swings. We diminish those aspects of our adolescence that we now think silly or embarrassing or alarming. We would rather not remember rebellion against parents or preoccupation with sex. We tell ourselves that when we were adolescents we were never controlled by hormones. In fact, the adult in us tends to make the real memories of adolescence quite vague. Did I really practise kissing on the back of my hand? Did I really rip up that class photo because the boy in it dated someone else? Did I really tell our parents those lies about going to the movies with friends of the same sex? What about those packs of cigarettes my parents knew nothing about?

Connecting with our own adolescence as it really was, and not as we have rewritten it, is the first and most important part of our research. When we can authentically recall and relive those years, then we'll be able to connect with the adolescents around us. For some, this is quite challenging. We see a society that is changing rapidly and we tend to think that teenagers today are very different from our day. Are they? I believe that the inner world of the adolescent is the same. The outer furnishings may change, but the inner needs, challenges, insecurities, priorities, are the same for every generation. The inner truth of your adolescence is the inner truth of the adolescent you will write for. It is the outer detail that you must add. Some writers can do this effectively. I think of Katherine Paterson, Jillian Sullivan, David Hill, Louis Sacher, Jerry Spinelli, William Taylor, Sherryl Jordan, or Margaret Mahy. They step across a generation gap with an easy stride. If you find this daunting, then you may wish to do a period piece set in your own time or earlier. As long as the inner truth of the adolescent's world is authentic, your reader will identify with it, whatever the time frame.

The main idea for the story is developing. This idea is the machine that drives the plot. It dictates what happens. But we won't get too far with plot development if we don't know our characters well. It is important to know precisely the age of our characters so that we can relate them to ourselves at the same age and to the young people we know and observe. Our characters, even the minor ones, must become so real to us that we know everything about them. We know what they look like, down to the last freckle. We can hear their voices in our heads.

How do our characters become real to us to this degree? It doesn't just happen. We have to work on them. I make biographical notes about each of my characters, when they were born, where, physical description, parents, likes and dislikes, hobbies, attitudes, positive traits, insecurities. I have the view that every human being is a mixture of strength and weakness; there are no 100 percent baddies or goodies in life. Saints do sneaky things, and habitual criminals make donations to charity. That's life. That's real. As I construct each character on paper, so does each come to life in my head as a balanced human being, full of potential.

Now, you can go to the paperback section in any airport bookstore and find a fast read in which there are no authentic characters. The people in these books are simple shapes, furniture for a sensational plot. We don't know them. We don't care about them. They have no real voice. All their dialogue is interchangeable.

As we develop our characters, and become aware of their voices, we will hear them talking in different ways. Everyone has a natural speech pattern that is as individual as fingerprints. Dialogue varies with each character. Sentence structure and length, repeated phrases, hesitations, confidence or shyness, exclamations — these are all aspects of individual speech patterns. I need to know exactly how my character is going to converse with others. I make notes on the bio sheet to remind me. Does my character's speech get muddled in moments of tension? Can my character be a bit manipulative, always looking out for number one? Is my character at times a know-it-all who doesn't like to be wrong? Does he or she tend to be a good leader? Or one who always defers to a leader? My character's personality will affect the way he or she speaks.

As our characters develop, so will our plots. Characters tend to feed a plot and sometimes they will dictate it.

Special issues with novels

Let me sidetrack a little here and talk about an aspect of young adult fiction that I find quite disturbing. I'm talking about 'bleak books'. I can only guess that many authors see adolescence as a bleak time, full of personal heartache, family problems, social challenges, a time that needs advice in the form of earnest sympathy and messages of hope.

Well, adolescence is difficult — at times. At times, it is also a blast. It's a time of far-out humour, close friendships, experiments, glorious highjinks, celebrations, and wonderful idealism. The mood swings go way up and way down. Do we honestly think that a teenager in the trough of a mood swing is going to feel better reading a depressing book?

Most of my books do have messages in them but I have two rules: no dumping on my readers, and no preaching. The difference between messages and preaching is the difference between showing and telling. In showing, the author can show the choices available and the effect of those choices. In telling, the author tells the reader what he or she should believe. It is not advisable to 'should' on readers. It turns them off. I firmly believe that my first duty to my reader is to entertain. Isn't that what we all ask of a book?

Okay, so no bleak books. We present a balanced picture and our plot is developing nicely. We've done our research. We've made notes about our characters, their actions and reactions. We think we're ready to start because we've got a good beginning and the rest will just follow, won't it? No! It's amazing how many writers begin a novel without first planning it from beginning to end. For an experienced writer, just sitting down and writing might work; for most of us, it doesn't. I would no more start a novel without a plan than I would have a house built without a plan. People have different work methods at the planning stage. My method usually consists of an outline of each chapter.

You may ask, how do you know what to put in each chapter? Let's go back to the main idea, the storyline. That's the backbone of our story. Everything else, the sub-plots, the dramatic movement of the novel, the interaction of the characters, hangs from that backbone. If I have some action that is not connected to the main storyline, I get rid of it. I find that in a historical novel or a fantasy novel, both of which require a lot of research, I want to put in all my research, whether it's relevant or not. I have to curb this tendency. I put in only the research material that is relevant to the story. The rest is discarded.

Now, may I say a few words about voice? By voice, I'm not talking about dialogue. I refer to the way we, as authors, tell our story. Is it going to be a first person narrative? Third person? Is it going to have a one-person point of view? Will it be told through the eyes of several people? Or will it be told from God's eye, looking down on all that happens? What tense will you use? The present, with everything happening as the reader reads? Or the past?

Having made these decisions, you can now ask yourself: how will I tell this story? Will I have the relaxed chatty style of one of the characters? Will I talk directly to the reader? Or perhaps, if this is a fantasy story, I could use the more formal and distant language of myth. I must find a voice for the narrative and I must remain true to it.

Earlier, I mentioned ideas as though they fell out of the sky. Sometimes they do just that. Usually, we have to search for them. Most of us have excellent ideas in the library of our own experience. Or maybe someone close to us has had an experience that will make a good novel. Failing that, we can try looking in newspapers. It has been said that in every newspaper there are at least eight good ideas for a story.

History is rich in ready-made plots, but be prepared for a lot of research. It's not simply a matter of researching the actual event, but also the background material. Cultural differences exist not just between ethnic groups; they also exist between then and now.

Fantasy is the most difficult genre because it has to work as reality. Some think that fantasy is separate from reality. It's not. It's an extension of it. Fantasy has to work logically, if it's to be convincing. This means more research. I lived through weeks of quantum physics, chaos theory and multiple realities in the planning of *Starbright and the Dreameater*. A few weeks after it was published, the film *The Matrix* was released. Someone had been doing the same kind if research, but had written it into a different story. In *Starbright* I also researched old messianic myths, plucking from them the common attributes: a hero who is pre-pubescent, born of a virgin, destined to be a saviour of his people. But in *Starbright*, the hero is a girl living here and now. My other sci-fi fantasy *Ticket to the Sky Dance* involved research into alternative medicine and human energy fields, as well as some alarming reading about missing street children in Brazil.

Well, I've planned my novel, I've lived it for several months and now it's finished. As every author knows, writing has a strong exhibitionist streak. The moment we type in that last word, it shrieks, 'Send me to a publisher!' I turn deaf ears to the new novel's pleas and close it down on the computer for several weeks or months until I am no longer involved with it. Then I can seriously begin the final editing process. It's amazing how much work is needed on a book at this stage.

Finally, it is ready for the publisher, and I send it away knowing that it was as good as I could possibly make it. Of course, an editor may not see it that way, but at least I have the satisfaction of honouring an idea with the best of my ability.

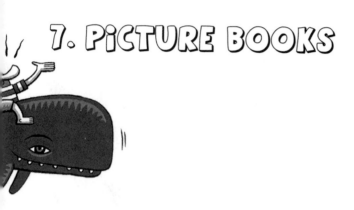

7. PICTURE BOOKS

What kind of story? Child-centred!

First, it is important that the picture book story be appropriate for the targeted age. Children of five years have different development and interests from seven-year-old children. We can't think in vague terms of a children's story. We must write for a specific readership, which is why writing for children requires more skill than writing for adults.

Second, children like to read about children their own age.

Third, children need to find affirmation in a story. The story should empower children in several ways: helping them to see themselves as successful readers; helping them to feel good about their ability to make cognitive connections and to solve problems; helping them to see their own worthiness in the characters. To this end, we do not have big people solving little people's problems.

Lastly, we need to be aware of the limitations of a young reader: we need to remember that the beginner reader does not have the experience of life and language to cope with certain literary styles. They find an open or inconclusive ending to a story bewildering. Stories should never have negative endings. It's okay to take the child into a tense plot, as long there is a happy ending.

Entertainment

The author's first duty is to entertain. Adults don't read dull and difficult material by choice, yet we often expect that of children.

Resist the temptation to preach at the young reader. All stories contain messages, but the messages are not the story. Didactic writing gets a negative response from children. On the other hand, they enjoy stories that are based on jokes or misunderstandings or family events. Look for a simple, child-centred plot that has a well-defined beginning, middle and end. Think visually. Much of the story will be told by the illustrations.

Humour is important. Not all stories lend themselves to laughter, but do remember that favourite books are usually funny. Children love to laugh and they laugh more than adults. Humour also plays a part, in that it releases tension in a nervous or reluctant reader: no one can be tense while they are laughing.

Again, be aware of the age of the reader. A five-year-old usually likes slapstick humour. The seven-year-old is looking for puns and word jokes. I developed a habit of putting a twist or joke at the end to encourage children to read to the last page. Although this is not essential, do make sure you have a strong, positive ending to your story.

Don't worry about vocabulary or syntax. An experienced editor will take care of that for you. Use simple, conversational English and, if you can, include some words that will delight children. Avoid rhyme because that usually makes language complex, but you can use rhythm, joke words, colourful words that describe noise or action, dialogue. Remember that a story is like music; it should not be written in a monotone, otherwise children will read it that way. Try to vary your language to make it interesting. You may find it helpful to think of 'telling the story on paper' using the kind of voice and words you would have if you were actually telling the story to a child. This usually results in a more relaxed and entertaining tale.

Common errors

- Lack of originality. Derivative works. Stories that have no heart — they have not engaged the author and will not engage the reader.

- Non-specific. Lack of awareness of the age of the reader. Vague idea of childhood.

- Cuddly or sentimental stories. Talking down to children. Using a baby-talk voice and words. 'Little boy/little girl'.

- Lack of understanding of the nature of a picture book. Too many words. A 32-page picture book should be less than 1000 words, probably 600–800.

- Too many message stories. Dull and worthy material. First duty is to entertain.

- Failure to realise that fantasy must work as reality. It must be logical to the reader.

- Misuse of anthropomorphism.

- Rhyme. This is difficult and must be done well. It needs natural language and rhythm, and must scan.

8. PLAYS

Plays extend the student's experience of literacy in an entertaining and non-threatening way. Like reading a big book, a play is also group activity — a smaller group of children who share a story by taking separate parts.

The student doesn't have to read the entire story. He or she receives the pleasure of the entire story by owning one of the characters. The concept of 'owning' is important here. Children readily move into role-playing and in doing so, they tend to leave themselves behind. In becoming a character in a play, the reader will step away from reading as 'hard work' and will forget the accompanying fear of failure. Any errors and mis-cues tend to be the responsibility of the character rather than the child. This is an important aspect of drama in the classroom. It helps to free the less-confident reader.

We know that reading skills are sometimes taught in ways that are not child-centred. The child may learn to read but will not learn to love reading if the exercise is dull and difficult and without meaning.

Plays are child-centred. They cater for the young child's readiness to act out a role. Children are much less inhibited

than adults at doing this, especially when they are with their peer groups. We are, in effect, using natural child-play to give meaning to the exercise of learning to read.

Plays in the classroom

I began writing simple plays for the classroom in the mid-1960s. Most of these were published in the New Zealand Education Department's *School Journal*, and some were reprinted in school magazines in New South Wales and Victoria, Australia. But it wasn't until we were putting together the Story Box reading programme in the late 1970s that I went into schools and worked the plays with students. They taught me a huge amount about writing plays for early reading, and I was never in any doubt about what worked and what didn't. Children let me know when they find my writing boring.

But there were also many positive experiences and one that still fills me with awe happened in 1971. I was in a country school in a small New Zealand town. A generous teacher had lent me her class of seven- and eight-year-olds so that I could try out some Story Box manuscripts. These stories were at early-fluency to mid-fluency levels so I had not paged them out in dummy books with rough illustrations. They were simply typed on foolscap paper.

The last story was a play. It was at early-fluency level, a simple repetitive play about a hole in a submarine. (It was inspired by the story of the little Dutch boy who put his finger in the wall of the dyke.) It went like this:

'Captain, oh Captain! There is a hole in our submarine!'
'A hole?'
'Yes, Captain, a hole! The water's coming in and we can't swim. Captain, what shall we do?'
The captain tells the first mate that he must put his finger in the hole. That's all right, but soon the second mate comes in.
'Captain, oh Captain! The hole is getting bigger.'
'Bigger?'
'Yes, bigger. The water's coming in and we can't swim. Captain, what shall we do?'

The second mate is told to put his hand in the hole. But the hole gets bigger. The engineer has to put his elbow in the hole, then the radio operator has to put his foot in the hole.

Finally, the cook has to sit in the hole — which isn't much fun in Arctic seas — but it is the cook who saves the submarine.

Well, I read the play to the class and then asked for volunteers to act it. The adrenalin was running high and there was a forest of hands and clicking fingers. One tall blond boy was particularly keen to be the captain. Since he had not been particularly active in the other stories, I called him to the front first. As I did so the teacher, who was sitting to one side of the room, rose out of her chair, paused and then sat down again. I chose the rest of the crew, gave each actor a typed copy of the play and away they went. The audience loved them, and the actors responded by shouting out the parts. The tall blond captain made a few mistakes but like the others, he was surfing on a wave of class applause and when the play ended, he wanted to read it again.

So they read it again — really hamming it up and this time adding a few actions. At the end of the second reading, the audience enthusiasm was chaotic and I lost control. The teacher came through the maze of noisy bodies and put her face close to my mine. She pointed to the grinning blond captain and said in my ear, 'He can't read.'

I don't need to say more about that experience except to say that it took me back to the child I was, who struggled with reading and who at almost nine years of age was functionally a non-reader. Then the picture book about Ping the little duckling was put on my desk and the entire process took on meaning. I so lost myself in that story that I forgot I couldn't read.

Suggestions for writing plays

Now let's look at the construction of sound or radio plays as opposed to stage plays. Stage plays that require actions also have their place, but they usually require more advanced skills. Lines need to be learned so that the actor can also concentrate on movement. Stage plays, to my mind, are not an important part of learning to read, whereas sound plays — or Readers' Theatre — are.

What are my general guidelines for writing sound plays?

1. Humour. I've tried writing straight drama and it doesn't work as well with young readers. Laughter is a valuable aid to reading in that it releases tension and creates a feeling of pleasure. I also try to put a satisfying snappy ending to a play to give the last laugh and make the comedy complete.

2. The play needs pace. It should be economically told in simple language, with a well-defined beginning, middle and end.

3. Sentence structure is varied but sentences should never be too long. Because a play is all dialogue, the strict rules of narrative need not apply. I try to model complete sentences but at times of tension or excitement, it's okay to use incomplete sentences and exclamations, as long as they have an exclamation mark after them.

4. A sound play should not have non-spoken directions in it. Young readers have difficulty distinguishing directions from speech. They will read stage directions in stage plays and in sound plays will read voice directions. For example, suppose I have the following two lines.

    > *First Robot: (whispers) I've lost my voice.*

    > *Second Robot: (shouts) Let me help you find it!*

    Young actors are likely to read this exchange as:

    > *First Robot: Whispers I've lost my voice.*

    > *Second Robot: Shouts let me help you find it.*

Voice directions could be given, by printing the First Robot's words in a small point size, and making the Second Robot's words big and bold.

5. I usually have three to five characters in a sound play. Having only two characters places a burden on the readers. Three is all right if the play is very short and/or simple. Over five characters can be confusing for listeners if the work is recorded and played back.

6. I try to make the characters' parts more or less equal. Having said that, I will sometimes have an interesting character with a less challenging part — this for a struggling reader. It is important that the smaller or simpler part has high entertainment value so that the reader's self-esteem is not threatened.

7. The characters need to use each other's names frequently to avoid confusion of voices.

8. With sound plays there is scope for a wider range of fantasy characters and action than would be possible with stage plays. As a writer, I'm aware that the dialogue needs to describe the setting and action of the play, and this needs to be done in a natural manner.

9. Because I need to avoid writing directions, I try to put all sound effects into speech. For example, someone might say: 'The motor's making a funny noise. Dubbitty-dong. Dubbitty-dong.' Or: 'The wind turned my umbrella inside out. Whee-ee! Whee-ee! Whump!'

10. In the simpler plays I try to stay with decodable language, that is, words that can easily be sounded out letter by letter, syllable by syllable. This is for auditory readers who need to hear the parts of a word.

11. It can be helpful to have the names of the parts colour-coded for easy recognition. This means that the young actor doesn't have to grope through the list of names to find her or his part.

12. In a story book, the text is usually broken by illustration. In the layout of a play we can have unbroken text on the outer edges of the spread — again, to avoid confusion and aid fluency. The illustration can then be in the middle of the spread.

The benefits of sound or radio plays for young students

As I mentioned in the chapter on writing for early reading, plots and themes that affirm the child are important. I try to use situation humour rather than put-down humour, but if the laughter is at someone's silliness, then the characters must be adults. We do not laugh at children.

Most of the plays I write have messages and you don't have to scratch far to find them, but a message is not the reason for the existence of the play. If we write with the intention to instruct, our play is likely to turn out dull and didactic.

I consider the most important part of the play is its ongoing life as inspiration for the student's own writing. Generally, young children do not have the experience of life and language to write creative stories and plays. Their writing is usually derivative. By giving them ideas and structures based on these plays, plus a little assistance, they can write their own sound or stage plays. Therefore, each play needs to be open to innovation and provide a springboard for classroom play writing.

9. POETRY

Poetry is an expansive word that covers rhymes, blank verse, haiku, sonnets, odes, jingles, limericks and more. You can fill a page with a list of poetic shapes and sizes that come under the general heading of poetry.

Each form has its own disciplines. Each conveys meaning in distilled language, with a few words carrying a lot of content. When we read our favourite poets, we are soon aware how poetry will move us profoundly. The language is usually simple, but the words are carefully chosen to take us beyond their literal meaning. The way words lie against each other, the way they sound, their rhythm and pacing, can unwrap in us unexpected responses. Many of us will agree that we get more 'Ah yes!' moments from reading good poetry than from prose. We can be surprised into laughter by a clever limerick, sigh at the beauty of a fine metaphor, or feel the heart move like a galloping horse to some Victorian ballad.

Our love of poetry probably began in the classroom, or even before that, with nursery rhymes. Most of us, at an early age, tried to write our own verse. The only scraps of writing that have survived from my childhood are rhyming verses influenced by people like A.A. Milne, Edward Lear and Mother Goose nursery rhymes. Looking back on my early efforts, I realise that much of my verse was autobiographical. Putting experience into rhyme, with a few character changes, removed the actions from me and offered what seemed a suitable disguise. For example, at ten, I had a rhyming poem published in the children's page of the *Southern Cross* newspaper. It concerned a boy called Willie who stole money from his mother's purse to buy sweets, and was eventually caught:

> *Willie stammered for words. He could find no excuse.*
> *Twas then that Mum's hairbrush came into use.*

When I read poetry written by children, I often see the same connection — experience camouflaged as fiction — and often the message is in rhyme.

Why are we so disposed to rhyme? I haven't the faintest idea. But I do know that almost as soon as we can talk, we start echoing words. A three-year-old granddaughter was in her high chair, eating bread and cheese. Aware that she had an audience, she turned the meal into a performance: 'Cheesey-weezey, bready-weddy.' She stuffed the last bit into her mouth. 'All gone. Deady-weddy.'

That rhyming instinct in the child stays the journey into adulthood, and when we decide to write for children, it will emerge with a flourish.

Poetry for and by children

Every year I read 250–300 manuscripts for a children's picture book award, and each year about a quarter of the stories are in rhyming verse. Unfortunately, only one has ever made the short list. Most of the stories would have been much better written in prose.

Why is a rhyming story so difficult to do well? Here are the most common reasons for failure.

The main problem is that language is usually distorted to fit the rhyme. Extra phrases are added. Sentence sequencing

can be back to front. Rhythm is uneven. A simple story that would be fine in prose for pre-school children ends up as a long, convoluted rhyme with difficult vocabulary.

If you want to write rhyming stories, read the published writers who do it well, beginning with A.A. Milne, through to New Zealand writers such as Margaret Mahy and Lynley Dodd. Note the following:

1.   The language is simple, clever and never forced.

2.   The plot has charm and originality.

3.   Sentence structure is logical.

4.   The rhythm has a regular, unbroken beat.

5.   When you have finished reading the rhyming story, you know absolutely that it is right and that it would not be as effective in prose.

Remember that young readers also enjoy poetry that doesn't rhyme. A poem can be like a torch illuminating one special scene, one profound thought or moment. Poems may bring young people to discovery of themselves or the world. If the poet is not hampered by the need to find rhyming words, the created work can come from a deeper place of the heart, and can therefore speak at the same level to the reader.

Poetic language at its best is simple, yet rich, and layered with meaning. It is a vehicle for feeling, and its touch can be wild and passionate, or cool and elegant. It usually brings the reader to a new place of understanding.

When children write poetry that is free from the restraints of rhyme, the effect can contain both beauty and wisdom. I still have a poem sent to me a long time ago by an 11-year-old poet who likened an argument to stormy weather. She described thunder, lightening, heavy rain and finally, the emerging rainbow. Her last line was: 'A rainbow is a bridge that cannot be burned.'

Subject matter for poems is everywhere. Here are a few lines, also about the weather, that describe the quality of light in Wellington, New Zealand, after a storm:

> *Light dances on hills and office windows*
> *and shakes its skirts over the harbour*
> *in a wild fandango that attracts*
> *the pale moths of yachts in droves.*

I think that simplicity is the key to the kinetic energy of a poem. That is good news for a new writer. If you want to write poetry for children, and have difficulty with rhyme, push the rhyming instinct aside and put your thoughts into beautiful dense language. You may be agreeably surprised at the result.

10. PUTTING ON YOUR EDITOR'S HAT

The author in you has done the first draft of a story and is feeling pleased with the result, but you know that some editing needs to be done. Editing is a learned skill and new authors sometimes feel a little daunted by the prospect. Here are some time-tested hints that may help you.

1. Have you included all the information that the story needs? When the story is vivid in our mind, we can sometimes neglect to put important details on paper.

2. Is the information in the right order? For example, we don't bring in a description of the character near the end of a story. Nor do we introduce things as coincidence. The important elements of the plot need to be introduced early so that when they are needed, they are a natural and real element of the story.

3. Next we check our beginnings and endings. There is always a tendency to work our way towards the real beginning and then, when the story has gained pace, we carry on after the right ending. Does your beginning

seem a little slow? If so, try starting the story with action or dialogue, to grab the reader's interest. In the first sentences of a story, you need to give your reader a sense of place, and also information about the characters, but this can be threaded into dialogue and/or action. To begin a story with long chunks of narrative description can be boring for a young reader. As for the ending, look at the plot and the conflict or problem that gets solved. Usually the end of the story comes soon after that resolution.

4. Every story has a plot. A plot is what happens in a story and as already mentioned, the plot is about some kind of problem that gets solved. The story builds up to this with an increase in tension. The peak of that tension can be called the main dramatic moment. How have we dealt with the main dramatic moment in our story? Have we made it exciting for the reader? Or have we dismissed it in a few words?

5. Dialogue. There is something in us that looks for dialogue in a story. Children especially will want conversations in their books and will reject stories that don't have enough 'talking' in them. How have we used dialogue in our stories to give them interest and push the plot? When writing for early reading, we need to say simply who is speaking — they said, she asked, he replied. But when writing for fluent readers, we can say much more by using body language with dialogue. For example: 'Peter rubbed the back of his neck. "No, honestly, I really mean it".'

6. Pacing. A story is like music. It has movement and moods — fast and slow, gentle and hard, words that have rhythm, words that clash in discord. You can say a lot about what is going on in the story by the words you choose and the length of sentences. Long sentences slow a story to a relaxed pace. Short sentences give a sense of tension and breathlessness. If we tell a story all in the same way, it can sound to the readers like a monotone.

7. Cliches. Some words and phrases are used so often they become almost weightless. If we spot a well-worn expression in a story, we should try to find a new way of saying what we mean.

8. Grammar. When writing books that will be used in schools, try to keep to standard English language of the kind that children are expected to learn. There is, however, a difference between the language of narrative that obeys all the rules, and the language of dialogue that has freedom of expression. People rarely speak in perfect sentences and if they do so in our story, the result is likely to sound unnatural. Always use natural language in dialogue.

9. Spelling, punctuation, syntax. At this stage we look through our stories to check these three. We are not only concerned with correct spelling, punctuation and the arrangement of words, we are also looking for repetition. Do we have too many sentences structured

the same way? Do we have words that clash or are repeated, when we don't want that effect? Remember that every story written for children will be read aloud. Read your story out loud. Words are different to the ear and to the eye.

10. Is the story lacking humour? All stories will elicit emotions from a reader, making them happy, excited, sad, scared, indignant, or reflective. Often an author will forget that the most popular stories are those that make children laugh. Even a serious story can have its funny moments.

While a picture book story can be written in a week or less, the editing process goes on for months. I cannot say too often, don't be tempted to send your story to a publisher after the first edit. Keep it on your computer and go back to it at regular intervals. You will do a lot of fine-tuning over several weeks, deleting words that are superfluous, rearranging sentences and substituting words that are better suited to the intended meaning. This final polishing creates a professional story that will take the eye of an editor in a publishing office.

I keep a story on the computer for two or three months while I refine and polish it. While my second draft is the big edit, I know that I am not able to complete the job while I am still emotionally involved with what I have written. When I am detached, I can see more clearly what I have written, and what further changes need to be made.

11. PRESENTATION

Years ago, I was shown around a busy publishing office in New York, and introduced to many of the staff. I met a young woman, fresh out of college, who was a new assistant editor. It was her job to evaluate incoming manuscripts and determine which should go further to an editor's desk.

This assistant had two stacks of large yellow envelopes beside her desk, each about as high as the seat of her chair. Known as 'the slush pile', this was the amount of mail she had to go through in a week. Of course she didn't have time to read it all. She would look at the first page of a manuscript or, if the writing did not show promise, only the first paragraph. If the manuscript was poorly presented, with wrong spacing and incorrect paragraph indentation, faded or small print, or sloppy appearance, it was not read at all. The editor who was showing me around the office said that a quick glance determined whether a work came from a professional writer or an amateur.

WARNING: Make sure your manuscript is well presented.

In past years, as a judge of literary competitions, as a part-time worker in a publishing house and as an established writer trying to help newcomers, I've read thousands of manuscripts, and it has been a rare thing to see a story correctly submitted.

Manuscripts come in with single spacing, no paragraph indentation, narrow margins, odd fonts, rings of tea and coffee stains and, sometimes, hand written. An interesting story of pioneer farming was delivered in 11 exercise books written in faded pencil: although it was engaging material, it was never published.

These days, many people are writing and hoping to be published. Unless your manuscript looks professional, it is unlikely to be read. This is a hard fact. I don't intend to go into details of style and layout here, but will offer a few practical hints.

Read! A new writer who doesn't read the kind of books s/he wants to write is handicapped. How else can we know the market? Read the popular books and learn from the authors. How do they capture and hold the reader's interest? How do they use the tools of language? Look at grammar, punctuation, layout — what can you learn?

You can borrow from a library a book of style and grammar that will show you how to present your story. Better still, buy one, it's a good investment.

If you have written a picture book text DON'T get it illustrated. Publishing houses have their own stable of professional illustrators and they reserve the right to choose the appropriate artist for a work. Besides, if the story is accepted, by the time it has been edited and the layout done, the paging will be quite different.

Always put a cover sheet on your story. The information on the cover sheet is brief but contains everything an editor needs to know: title of story, genre, number of words, your name and contact details, and the name of your agent if you have one. If a story comes back from a publisher and you want to send it out again, reprint it if it looks tired, and certainly give it a fresh cover sheet.

Do not send a long letter with your manuscript. Publishers agree that usually, the longer the letter, the worse the

manuscript. This may sound harsh but there is no reason why you should explain the story in the covering letter. The story will explain itself.

Do not ask an editor to give a critique of your story. That is not the editor's job.

Be sure that your work is as good as you can get it before you submit it to a publisher. If it is rejected and you later see faults in it, it is unlikely that the publisher will want to see it again.

Your library will have writers' handbooks that give advice and list available markets. You may also wish to join your national writers' group (like the New Zealand Society of Authors) or an international group like SCBWI (Society of Children's Book Writers and Illustrators) that gives valuable support and publishing information.

Many publishers accept only manuscripts submitted by agents, but it is not easy for a new author to find an agent, since most agents only take published authors. How do you get around this Catch 22 situation? You can try writing for children's magazines and radio. Once you have established a list of acceptances, you can approach an agent.

Epilogue

Wherever the stories of your heart take you, you will love the journey. There will be times of frustration when you feel like a surfer with a board under your arm, gazing at a flat sea; at other times you will be swept away on a wave of inspiration that defies description.

I know many writers, but I have yet to meet one who has given up writing to do something else.

May you be afflicted with the same addiction.

ACKNOWLEDGEMENTS

The Storylines Children's Literature Charitable Trust extends grateful thanks to Joy Cowley for her generous gift of this manuscript to the Trust for publication.

Royalties from the sale of this North American edition will go towards the Trust's continuing work, through events, awards, publications and advocacy, to promote children's literature and literacy in New Zealand.

Joy's standing as a leading children's author, particularly in the field of educational books, is widely recognised both in her own country and overseas. Less well known outside literary and educational circles is her generosity, of which her commitment as a Storylines Trustee and this Storylines publication, written to provide aspiring and emerging authors with invaluable tools, are but two examples.

We are also hugely grateful to the following people who also provided their skills and services *pro bono* to assist the production, promotion and distribution of the book: illustrator Fraser Williamson for his delightful line drawings; designer Kate Walters; Trustee Tessa Duder for editing assistance; Kate Thompson and Mary de Ruyter for help with proof-reading; and Trustee Peter Dowling for overseeing the whole production.

For more information about the work of the Storylines Trust, both in its work in New Zealand and as the New Zealand Section of IBBY (International Board on Books for Young People), please visit the website.

www.storylines.org.nz

0 8 | 11

DK READERS

Pre-level 1

Fishy Tales
Colorful Days
Garden Friends
Party Fun
In the Park
Farm Animals
Petting Zoo
Let's Make Music
Meet the Dinosaurs
Duck Pond Dip
My Dress-up Box
On the Move

Snakes Slither and Hiss
Family Vacation
Ponies and Horses
My Day
John Deere: Busy Tractors
LEGO® DUPLO®: On the Farm
Cuentos de Peces *en español*
Dias Ilenos de color *en español*
Star Wars: Blast Off!
Star Wars The Clone Wars: Don't Wake the
  Zillo Beast!

Level 1

A Day at Greenhill Farm
Truck Trouble
Tale of a Tadpole
Surprise Puppy!
Duckling Days
A Day at Seagull Beach
Whatever the Weather
Busy Buzzy Bee
Big Machines
Wild Baby Animals
A Bed for the Winter
Born to be a Butterfly
Dinosaur's Day
Feeding Time
Diving Dolphin
Rockets and Spaceships
My Cat's Secret
First Day at Gymnastics
A Trip to the Zoo
I Can Swim!
A Trip to the Library
A Trip to the Doctor
A Trip to the Dentist
I Want to be a Ballerina
Animal Hide and Seek
Submarines and Submersibles
Animals at Home
Let's Play Soccer
Homes Around the World

LEGO® DUPLO®: Around Town
LEGO® City: Trouble at the Bridge
LEGO® City: Secret at Dolphin Bay
LEGO® Pirates: Blackbeard's Treasure
Star Wars: What is a Wookiee?
Star Wars: Ready, Set, Podrace!
Star Wars: Luke Skywalker's Amazing Story
Star Wars: Tatooine Adventures
Star Wars The Clone Wars: Watch Out for
  Jabba the Hutt!
Star Wars The Clone Wars: Pirates... and
  Worse
Power Rangers: Jungle Fury: We are the
  Power Rangers
Indiana Jones: Indy's Adventures
John Deere: Good Morning, Farm!
A Day in the Life of a Builder
A Day in the Life of a Dancer
A Day in the Life of a Firefighter
A Day in the Life of a Teacher
A Day in the Life of a Musician
A Day in the Life of a Doctor
A Day in the Life of a Police Officer
A Day in the Life of a TV Reporter
Gigantes de Hierro *en español*
Crías del mundo animal *en español*

A Note to Parents

DK READERS is a compelling program for beginning readers, designed in conjunction with leading literacy experts, including Dr. Linda Gambrell, Distinguished Professor of Education at Clemson University. Dr. Gambrell has served as President of the National Reading Conference, the College Reading Association, and the International Reading Association.

Beautiful illustrations and superb full-color photographs combine with engaging, easy-to-read stories to offer a fresh approach to each subject in the series. Each DK READER is guaranteed to capture a child's interest while developing his or her reading skills, general knowledge, and love of reading.

The five levels of DK READERS are aimed at different reading abilities, enabling you to choose the books that are exactly right for your child:

Pre-level 1: Learning to read
Level 1: Beginning to read
Level 2: Beginning to read alone
Level 3: Reading alone
Level 4: Proficient readers

The "normal" age at which a child begins to read can be anywhere from three to eight years old. Adult participation through the lower levels is very helpful for providing encouragement, discussing storylines, and sounding out unfamiliar words.

No matter which level you select, you can be sure that you are helping your child learn to read, then read to learn!

DK

LONDON, NEW YORK, MUNICH,
MELBOURNE, AND DELHI

Series Editor Deborah Lock
U.S. Editor Shannon Beatty
Designer Rosie Levine
Production Editor Sean Daly
Picture Researcher Rob Nunn
Jacket Designer Natalie Godwin

Reading Consultant
Linda Gambrell, Ph.D

First American Edition, 2011
Published in the United States by
DK Publishing
375 Hudson Street, New York, New York 10014

11 12 13 14 15 10 9 8 7 6 5 4 3 2 1
001-182472-August 2011

Published in Great Britain by Dorling Kindersley Limited.

A catalog record for this book is available
from the Library of Congress.

ISBN: 978-0-7566-8930-8 (paperback)
ISBN: 978-0-7566-8931-5 (hardcover)

DK books are available at special discounts when purchased in bulk
for sales promotions, premiums, fund-raising, or educational use.
For details, contact:
DK Publishing Special Markets
375 Hudson Street
New York, New York 10014
SpecialSales@dk.com

Printed and bound in China by L Rex Printing Co., Ltd.

The publisher would like to thank the following for their kind
permission to reproduce their photographs:
a=above, b=below/bottom, c=center, l=left, r=right, t=top

Alamy Images: D. Hurst 18fbr; Nikreates 19bc, 31br; Pegaz 20-21.
Corbis: Heide Benser 26-27; Randy Faris 4; Move Art Management
5. **Getty Images:** Fuse 10t; The Image Bank / John Kelly 19t; The
Image Bank / Martin Poole 16t; Lifesize / Yellow Dog Productions
18c, 32clb; Stockbyte / Steve Wisbauer 18br.

All other images © Dorling Kindersley
For further information see www.dkimages.com

Discover more at
www.dk.com

Contents

My Day

DK Publishing

Good morning!
I wake up and stretch.

arm

It's the start
of a new day.

I wash my face
and put on
my clothes.

T-shirt

 clothes

hanger

7

 breakfast

I sit down to eat my breakfast.

cereal

bowl

shoelaces

shoes

I put on my shoes
and my coat
for school.

coat

I play with the shapes at school.

shapes

square

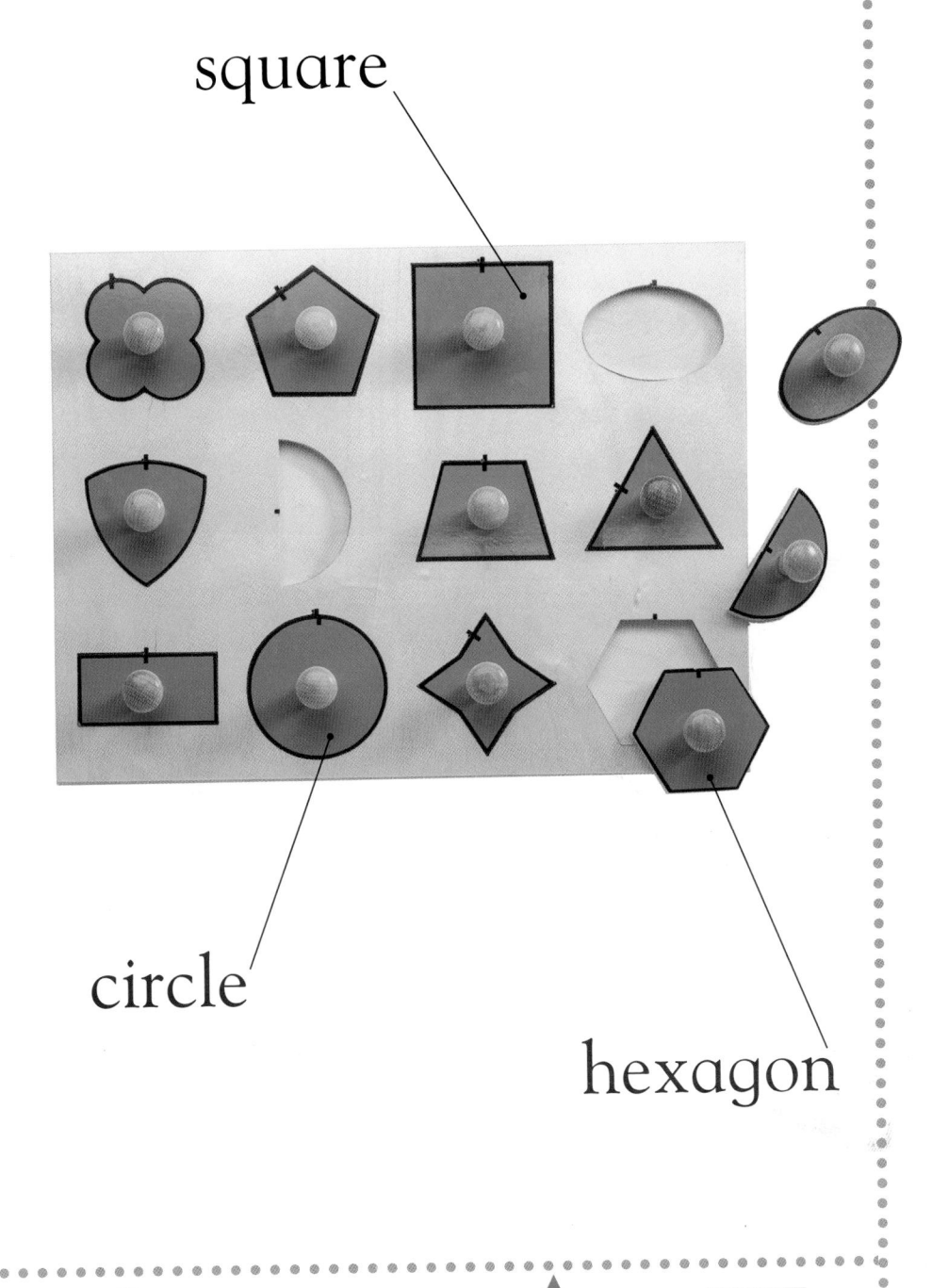

circle

hexagon

games

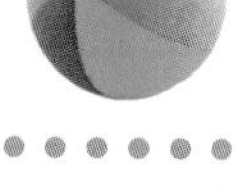

I learn games with my class.

It's lunchtime!

apple

water

I sit down
to eat my lunch.

 lunch

17

tricycle

playground

I ride and swing and
slide at the playground.

Good afternoon!

music

I jump around to music
before I go home.

I play with my toys
when I get home.

train

doll

ball

toys

peas

cook

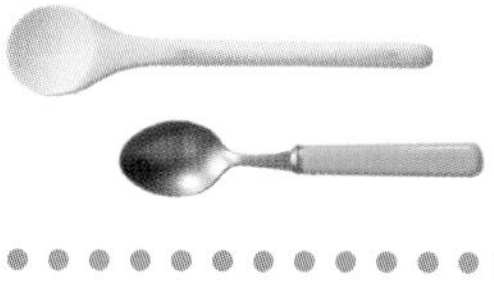

rice

I help
cook dinner.

I take a bath and brush
my teeth after eating
my dinner.

bathrobe

bathtime

toothbrush

book

pajamas

I put on my pajamas
and then read a book.

teddy bear

I get into bed.
It's the end of my day.

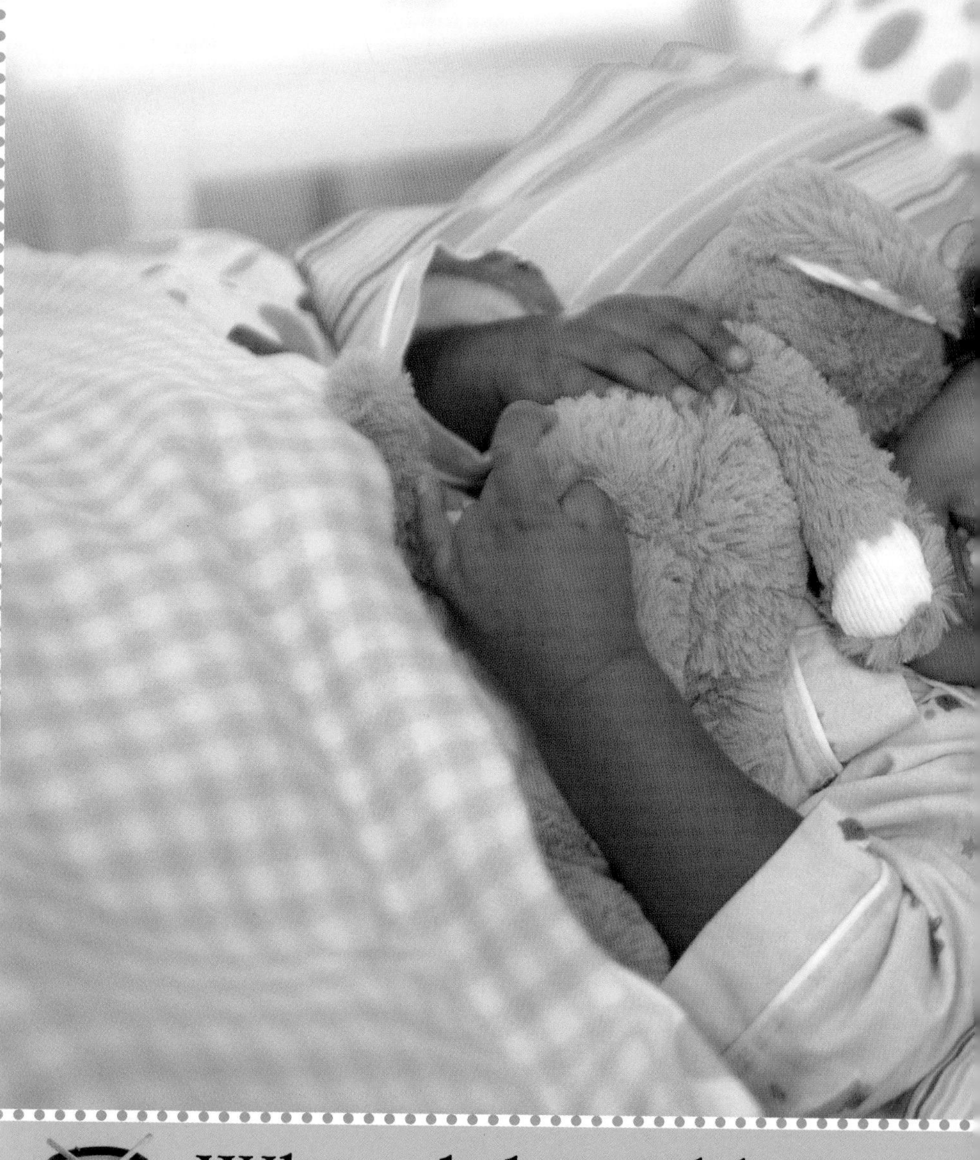

 What did you like

Goodnight!

doing today?

Glossary

 **Breakfast**
is the first meal
of the day.

 **Cook**
is to make food
ready for eating.

 **Lunch**
is a meal eaten in
the middle of the day.

Playground
is an outdoor place
where children play.

 **School**
is a building where
children go to learn.

Index